my garden

Wright Group

www.WrightGroup.com

 **Wright Group**

Send all inquiries to:
Wright Group/McGraw-Hill
P.O. Box 812960
Chicago, IL 60681

ISBN 978-0-07-658165-8
MHID 0-07-658165-9

4 5 6 7 8 9 DRN 16 15 14 13 12 11

J.M. Parramón
Irene Bordoy

my garden

There was once a girl named Maria, and she had three friends named John, Isabel and Peter.

Maria's grandfather was a gardener, and he took care of the flowers and plants in a very large garden.

Maria's grandfather loved to stroll in the garden, stopping here and there to look at the flowers.

One day, John, Isabel and Peter went with Maria to see her grandfather and visit the garden.

He taught them about roses,
daisies, gardenias…

…and fruit trees.

"You see?" he said, "This is an apple tree; this is a cherry tree; this is a pear tree."

Grandfather also showed them a pond with colorful goldfish and flowers called water lilies.

Then Grandfather,
John, Isabel, Peter and Maria
went into the greenhouse.

He said, "In here, the plants and flowers stay nice and warm, and they grow faster."

Grandfather explained
to John, Isabel, Peter and Maria
how plants and flowers grow.
"Look closely," he said,
"These are daisy seeds."

"When you put the seeds in a pot and wait a few days, each seed sprouts tiny roots.

"A few days more, and a little plant begins to grow.
Then ...

"…when a daisy plant has grown for a while, it is transplanted to a larger pot and watered…

…and when nice weather comes along, the flowers bloom."

Then Maria and her friends went to a terrace, and Maria said, "Now you know what MY GARDEN is like."